MARS AND VI

THE MEMORIES OF A GUNNER
210 BATTERY (WORCESTERSHIRE YEOMANRY)
53RD ANTI-TANK REGIMENT
ROYAL ARTILLERY TERRITORIAL ARMY

1937 to 1943

By
JACK CREED
with Robin Bird

BREWIN
BOOKS

First Published by
Brewin Books Ltd, Studley, Warwickshire
in March 2000
www.brewinbooks.com

© Jack Creed with Robin Bird 2000

All Rights Reserved

ISBN 1 85858 160 5

British Library Cataloguing in Publication Data
A Catalogue record for this book is available from the
British Library

Typeset in Palatino and
made and printed in Great Britain by
SupaPrint (Redditch) Ltd
Redditch, Worcestershire
www.supaprint.com

I dedicate this book to my dear wife
GLADYS MAY CREED
for without her interest
and support over many years
it would not come to have been written

R.I.P.

22nd December 1998

A WALK ALONG LIFE'S PATH

Are you going my way today?
Will you walk awhile, pray,
Teach me how to live again,
To enjoy a droplet of rain,
As it falls upon your cheek,
Pray teach me, how to speak,
Kindly to each soul, that I meet,
As I walk upon the street,
Of life's sometime troubled path,
And finally, teach me how to laugh.

Gladys & Jack Creed

CONTENTS

Pre-Enlistment		8
CHAPTER ONE	Enlistment and Camp	9
CHAPTER TWO	Mobilisation and Training	13
CHAPTER THREE	With the B.E.F. in France January to May 1940	16
CHAPTER FOUR	Action at Wormhoudt and the Retreat to Dunkirk May 1940	18
CHAPTER FIVE	The Regiment Reforms	25
CHAPTER SIX	Hospital and Romance	28
CHAPTER SEVEN	178 Battery and Discharge	31
CHAPTER EIGHT	Civilian Life and Return to Wormhoudt	34
APPENDIX 1	The Worcestershire Yeomanry 1920-1942	36
APPENDIX 2	Weapons and Small Arms 1939	38
APPENDIX 3	The 2lb Anti-Tank Gun	39
APPENDIX 4	Shot and Shell	42
APPENDIX 5	Insignia	43
APPENDIX 6	Conscription	44
APPENDIX 7	The German Soldiers Ten Commandmentsand the Waffen S.S. Oath	45
APPENDIX 8	Massacre at Wormhoudt	46
	Map	47
	Bibliography	48

Not to be maintained in duplicate. Army Form E 623 B.

TERRITORIAL ARMY.

IMMEDIATE AND IMPORTANT.—NOTICE TO JOIN.

No., Rank and Name _1464547 Gnr Creed J.R._

Unit ....

In accordance with an authority signed by the Secretary of State, you are hereby called up for service in accordance with the agreement entered into by you under Section 1S (2) (b) of the Territorial and Reserve Forces Act, 1907, and you are required to report immediately at _Drill Hall Morefield Road Kings Heath_

Should you not present yourself as ordered, you will be liable to be proceeded against.

Place _210th (Wor...._
                                              Adjutant.

Time _4-0. P.M_

Date _1-9-39_
                                              Unit.

N.B.—This notice to be sent by hand or by registered post in a plain envelope. (A.F. D419 will not be used.)

Battery Orders by Major J. K. Brodie, T.D., R.A., (T.A.)
Commanding 210th (Worcester Yeomanry) Anti-Tank Battery, R.A. (T.A.)

Annual Training.

1st BATTERY.—Training will take place at TRAWSFYNYDD, Wales, for those who have been warned by official notice to join (A.F.E. 654) from June 24th to JULY 8th.

2nd BATTERY.—Training will take place at PERDISWELL PARK, Nr. Worcester, from July 16th to July 30th.

Times of Parade.

1st BATTERY will parade at Battery Headquarters on Saturday, June 24th at 9 p.m. ready to move off. DRESS:—Service Dress with trousers for those in possession Battle Dress for those not in possession of Service Dress; Waistbelt; haversack, Webb battle. dress Tin, Greatcoat (to be carried).

ADVANCE PARTY will leave by road on June 22nd, parade at 4-30 a.m.

2nd BATTERY will parade at Battery Headquarters on Sunday July 16th at 8-45 a.m. DRESS:—As above. The Battery will proceed by road to PERDISWELL. Major J. T. K. KENRICK will be in command of this Battery throughout its training.

ADVANCE PARTY FOR 2nd BATTERY will leave on July 13th at 9 a.m. Every endeavour will be made to equip all ranks of 2nd Battery with Greatcoats before training, but if this is not possible men are warned to bring Mackintosh or Overcoat.

KIT BAGS AND LUGGAGE FOR 1st BATTERY must be at Battery Headquarters before 8 p.m. on June 24th; **2nd BATTERY** by 8-45 a.m. on July 16th.

Personal Equipment.

All ranks must bring with them clean change of underclothes, spare socks, knife, fork, spoon, razor, shaving gear, toothbrush, soap, towels. Bathing costumes and sports gear should be brought to camp. Health and Unemployment Insurance Cards must be brought with you to camp.
Leave can only be considered on the grounds of ill-health and applications must be supported by a Doctor's Certificate.

Marriage Allowance.

All married N.C.O's and men who have not given in details of their wives and families must hand them in to Battery office at once.

2nd Battery.

Drills of the 2nd Battery will continue during the time the 1st Battery is at Camp, on Mondays and Thursdays at 8 p.m. and on Sundays June 25th and July 2nd at 9 a.m. B.S.M. CLAPP will take charge of these parades.

(Sig:d) J. K. BRODIE, Major, R.A., (T.A.)
Commanding 210th Worcester Yeomanry Anti-Tank Battery, R.A., (T.A.)

KINGS HEATH,
16/6/39.

Pre-Enlistment

How I remember those nostalgic memories pre to enlistment to the TA in 1937/38. The phoney war period when everyone wondered if we would soon be at war with Germany.

I remember it well when my school pal and I decided to join the TA. The Drill Hall was in Mossfield Road, Kings Heath, situated in a quiet road among small council houses. In we went into the nostalgic atmosphere of the wooden-floored drill hall, which was complete with Bar where we obtained a cool bottle of family ale or Export; after completing one's duties - I can taste it now.

Firstly we had to swear to be loyal to King and Country. Eventually we were issued with our thick battle dress uniforms, complete with boots, putties - which later changed to gaiters which went around the ankles. Kit bag complete with such things as blankets, house wife (sewing kit), brass button stick, and bag for the straw palliases.

And then we had our first taste of drill. Slope arms, order arms, stand at ease etc. We were now to be moulded into soldiers. I remember one glorious sunny day doing our first drill outside the drill hall, with our first and only 2lb anti-tank gun. The locals looking on and intrigued no doubt at us removing the wheels and getting the gun ready for action in about 29 seconds.

We were ready for our first TA Camp at Worcester. The sun always seemed to shine in those days.

CHAPTER ONE
Enlistment and Camp

By the middle of the 1930's it was becoming very clear that for the second time in some twenty years war with Germany was almost inevitable.
A former Rover Scout living in Birmingham I joined, in either late 1937 or early 1938, I am not clear about the exact date now some sixty years on, the Territorial Army. My Regiment was the Worcestershire Yeomanry which with the Oxfordshire Yeomanry then was part of the 100th, Field Artillery Brigade Royal Artillery. Both the Worcestershire and Oxfordshire Yeomanry Regiments had served through the 1914-1918 war as "horsed" Cavalry Regiments and had in 1922 been reorganised and converted to Artillery. The commanding officer of the regiment at this time was Lieutenant Colonel A.J. Muirhead.
My actual unit the Worcestershire Yeomanry then had two batteries, 210 which was the one I had joined in Birmingham and 397 based further afield in Kidderminster.
During 1938 the War Office decided to convert a number of units including my own from Field Artillery to Anti-Tank Artillery. Our 18lb guns, the mainstay of the Field Artillery during the First World War being replaced with new velocity 2lb Anti-Tank guns. With the change of role came a change of name so that we became the 53rd, (Worcestershire and Oxfordshire Yeomanry), Anti-Tank Regiment, Royal Artillery, Territorial Army.
Early in 1939 a further reorganisation and renaming took place as War became nearer. Now both parts of the regiment were split so that the Worcestershire Yeomanry became the 53rd, Worcestershire Yeomanry Anti-Tank Regiment Royal Artillery Territorial Army and the Oxfordshire Yeomanry became the 63rd, Oxfordshire Yeomanry Anti-Tank Regiment Royal Artillery Territorial Army. It was later under these names that both units were to see war service.
In July 1939 I attended what was to be the last pre-war "Camp" which the Regiment held. We travelled to Perdiswell Park near Worcester and slept in canvass Bell Tents of World War One vintage. These tents each held 8 men sleeping with our feet to the pole. Each very proud of ourselves we swaggered about in our uniforms

which then still included puttees. A friend and I bought riding crops from a local shop and with these thought that we were "real soldiers"!

During the camp we undertook gun drills on our new 2lb Anti-Tank guns which fired an armour piercing solid shot and stood guard with Lee-Enfield Rifles which we were also trained to use. Each of us had great pity for those who were responsible for the Boyes Anti-Tank Rifles for though our Lee-Enfields had a hard kick this was nothing compared to Boyes which had a kick comparable to that given by a Mule and often resulted in very sore shoulders. The very enjoyable camp over we returned to Birmingham.

Sports Day Perdiswell Park

Worcester - July 1939
Annual Camp Perdiswell Park

Perdiswell Park Worcester.
Territorials at Camp. J Coates second from right

Six 2lb Anti-Tank Guns at Perdiswell Park.

Tom Nichols after the war wearing the French policeman's hat at one of our reunions

Tom Nichols Wormhoudt Cemetery

CHAPTER TWO
Mobilisation and Training

On the 1st September 1939 I and every other member of the Territorial Army was called up for "war service". As directed by my "Call Up" document I reported to the Drill Hall in Mossfield Road, Kings Heath and was there for several nights sleeping on the floor. When I left home that day I wondered, as so many had before, "Would I return?".

The Senior Non-Commissioned Officer of my unit in Kings Heath was Battery Sergeant Major Swatton. He was a regular soldier of long service and a very strict but fair disciplinarian. Always immaculate in his uniform his boots and brasses shone as only those pre-ware regular soldiers did. At all time you could see yourselves in the shine of his boots.

I was told after the war by one of those involved that on the first night of mobilisation he swore the Head Quarters' clerks and others to secrecy with dire threats of retribution, "a guts for garters job", so I was told, then left the Depot for a time. When he returned it was with fish n' chip suppers for them all!

On the sunny Sunday morning of 3rd September 1939 at Kings Heath Drill Hall, we were paraded to listen to the Prime Minister Mr Neville Chamberlain, a former Lord Mayor of Birmingham, when he spoke on the wireless. He explained that were now at war with Germany. What thoughts went through my own mind at this I can't now recall.

The Prime Minister's speech over no, time was lost in moving away from Birmingham and the heavy air-raids that were expected to start at any moment.

Either later on that day, Sunday 3rd September 1939 or early the following morning, Monday 4th September 1939, we with our one or two 2lb Anti-Tank Guns, left Birmingham in the back of 15cwt trucks for the town of Wantage in Oxfordshire where we were to spend the next few months preparing for overseas service.

At this time Wantage was a very quaint town, its houses lacked electricity and were mainly lit by oil lamps which before the war had glowed each night in the windows. Now with the Blackout no lights anywhere were allowed to be seen. I and a number of others were billeted in the Church Hall, this being some 100 yards away from Battery Head Quarters where we paraded for drills and fatigues. We soon made friends with the local residents often being invited into their homes during the evenings and when off duty. The oil lamps which were their only source of light were put to very good use, our Army issue Woodbine Cigarettes being lit by just being touched to the glass-bowls over the lamps.

Through the lovely Autumn of 1939 and then on into the bitter Winter of 1939/40 we trained hard. The Regiment was being prepared for overseas' service being brought up to strength in both men, guns, transport and equipment of all kinds. Though we did not know it at the time almost all of this was to be left in France in May 1940. Some of the men who joined us at this time were volunteers others were either those called up under the "Militia Act" of May 1939, which provided for a limited period of compulsory military service for all those aged 20 to 24, or those called up since the war began under the National Services Act.

The country lanes of Oxfordshire were always busy with our vehicles roaring about on exercises and echoed to the orders, "Driver Stop! Halt! Action Rear," and, "Take Post". Orders being given and trucks would stop at once and we would jump out to get our guns into action in the very shortest possible time, taking the gun from off the hook on the truck, put the wheels down and use a handspike to traverse it before opening a rapid fire. We would then reverse the action and drive off to do the same somewhere else. This was fine in theory, but who though the idea up I would still like to know, as we found later from hard experience it was of no use in "action".

One of my most vivid memories of this time at Wantage and one which I still can't think how I got away with took place one night. Sitting on my bed I had been cleaning my equipment including boots, webbing and rifle when I realised that unless I hurried I would be late for guard duty and thus on a charge. Grabbing everything I charged out of the Church Hall, only when some way down the road to realise that I had left the bolt of my rifle on my bed. Panic set in and how. I had no time to return to collect this and without the bolt it was impossible for a rifle to be fired.

On falling in and being inspected for guard duty the order, "Ease Springs," was given. This required that the rifle bolt was moved "smartly" backwards and forwards so that it could be seen that no bullets were left in the rifle. This I had to mime and so hoped that the lack of my rifle bolt would not be noticed, how I sweated this out. Somehow, despite this I was chosen to be the "Stick Man", the smartest man on parade. The "Stick Man" was excused the actual duty though it was recorded as having been undertaken by him. My tasks for that night were now simple, act as "orderly" run messages and fetch and carry the "tea buckets" for those who actually were on guard. I managed to get a good night's sleep but still wonder if our Commanding Officer, Major Wiggin, ever found out what I had done.

CHAPTER THREE
With the B.E.F. in France
January to May 1940

During most of December 1939 a great deal of general "bull" polishing and cleaning everything in sight took place with great attention being paid to smartness on parade. This was the prelude to a full inspection of the Regiment by His Majesty the King on 2nd January 1940. This over the Regiment was declared fit in all respects for "war service" and orders were given for us to join the B.E.F. in France.

During the second week of January 1940 we said farewell to Wantage and left by truck for Southampton as part of the 48th, South Midland Division. We were the first Territorial Army Regiment to be sent overseas during World War Two. At Southampton the Regiment embarked in the docks, so soon to be heavily bombed, setting sail for Le Havre on what I seem to recall was the Isle of Man, a ship which in happier pre-war days had been used for the transport of holidaymakers.

We landed from our very overcrowded troopship in atrocious weather. This Winter of 1939 to 1940 was one of the most severe this century. Everywhere snow lay thickly on the ground and the cruel wind cut through our uniforms chilling us to the bone. After collecting our transport and guns we began to proceed along the long, straight roads of France and this continued for several days. At night we would stop when and where we could, often sleeping in barns. At long last we reached our destination very near to the frontier with Belgium called Henin-Leitard. This was a mining town in an area very familiar to those we had fought in World War One.

The aim of our move towards the frontier was to be ready to advance into Belgium, then still neutral, if and when the Germans attacked. Shades of World War One again. Our main role at this time was to provide Anti-Aircraft defence using the Bren Guns which were carried in most vehicles for this purpose.

Our journey was finally over and we soon settled into what was to be our home for some months. The troops billets were in the stables belonging to a coal mine and were situation at the end of a long cobbled and typically French yard. It was in this yard that we paraded for duty and for fatigues. Facilities were to say the least, very very basic. At night we slept on straw-filled palliases, then every morning had to wash and shave as Army orders decreed, this being in icy cold water which cut to the bone. Our toilet was that used previously by miners. This was open to the air above and just comprised a hole in the ground with screens around it to give some sense of privacy. It was in this that we squatted and tried hard not to fall down into the hole below. To use it in the weather conditions that then prevailed was always a very, very, very cold experience!

One of my main memories from this time in Henin-Leitard was being inspected in the yard by two Captains. One was Captain le Coutrier and the other Captain Cartland. He, Captain Cartland was the brother of the author Barbara Cartland and was in May 1940 to be tragically killed at Cassel near Wormhoudt when he tried to surrender to the Germans after we had been overrun by them.

Once our duties were over for the day and if we were not required for guard duty we were free to proceed into town provided we were smartly turned out and all webbing and boots were clean and polished.

It was here that in the bars and cafés our schoolboy French was put to good use. Though we had very little money, my pay as a Gunner at this time was only some 2/6 or 12_ pence in today's money per day, with the then rate of exchange being some 178 Francs to the Pound Sterling. We were still able to indulge in egg 'n' chips, the favourite food of the B.E.F. in two world wars and large bowls of black coffee and Cognac. These did much to warm us up.

Despite being very sternly warned of the dangers and consequences by the unit Medical Officer, the Black Cat, a place of ill-repute, was one of the main haunts of the unit off-duty. He, the medical officer, described us as "meat going into a mincing machine"! I leave the rest to your imagination.

I very well remember that one of my friends was taking out the daughter of the Concierge. Slipping out quietly one night he was stopped in his tracks when the girl's mother called out to him, "Monsieur. Vous avec ici tout suit." He did not know that she "fancied him too" and so certainly got a lot more than he bargained for! Though this was still the period of the Phoney War, rumours of spies and fifth columnists abounded, it was said that some German Paratroops had been dropped dressed as Nuns and were now behind us. As we tried to sleep each night this was interrupted by the sounds of shots with bullets flying about outside the stables. Possibly this might have been hunters or just people settling old pre-war scores?

CHAPTER FOUR
Action at last Wormhoudt and the Retreat to Dunkirk May 1940

They say that all good things must come to an end at some stage. For me and for 210 Battery as a whole this took place on the 10th May 1940 when Germany began to invade France, Belgium, Holland and Luxembourg. German planes began to bomb Henin-Leitard very early that morning, at the time we thought they were after our Battery Headquarters.

As had been planned many months before, now that German Troops were advancing into Belgium, the B.E.F. with my Regiment one of the first to do so, was able to cross the frontier to meet them. At first we were welcomed by throngs of Belgian civilians, this however soon changed as we neared the fighting and they were replaced by long, long lines of refugees, old and young, many on foot or in horse-drawn carts fleeing the advancing Germans. The movement of these refugees greatly impeded our own movements. Now we passed through many very heavily bombed towns and villages.

A small party had been left behind in Henin-Leitard. A friend, Tom Nichols later told me what happened. After most of us had left he was standing by the gate of our former barracks when a young Polish girl aged 12 or 13, looking very sad came up to him. Only the previous night I had been happily eating egg 'n' chips in her parents' house. The girl asked for me in French and said, "Where is the young soldier with glasses?" Tom told her that we had moved out only that morning and she went away. Looking back now some 60 years later I wonder if she survived and still lives there. It would be lovely to meet her again after all these years.

I have been told that as we advanced we shot down some 6 enemy aircraft in that one day but can't be sure of this. In theory, we were, on sighting an enemy aircraft, to jump out of our 15cwt trucks, set up our Bren Guns on their tripods and fire away. However, by this time we had done this the planes were long gone and I did not see any German planes brought down by our fire.

My main memories of this time are of always being tired and of the constant streams of refugees that came past us away from the fighting. The furthest point that we reached was near Waterloo where we were able to make a very, very welcome cup of tea and for the first time in several days I was able, at last, to take off my heavy Army boots and bathe my feet in a lovely ice-cold stream.

Though I did not know this at the time, the B.E.F. was successfully holding back the Germans but the French First Army under General Billote to our right could not do this and was forced to retreat. On the 16th May 1940 Lord Gort the commander of the B.E.F. gave orders for the B.E.F. to withdraw so that we would not be outflanked.

Our first news of what was happening was the arrival of a Despatch Rider on a motorbike either late on the 16th or early on the 17th May. He told us that the Germans were now very, very close and we had to move back, and fast, to avoid being trapped by them. This started a twenty day period of retreat that was not to end until we finally reached the beaches of Dunkirk.

We began to leapfrog backwards, taking up a position, staying there for a short time and then moving back again, many times by night to escape the German aircraft that during the day constantly flew overhead. At no time during the retreat did I see an aircraft from the R.A.F. Whenever we took up a position we were passed by the infantry of many different regiments including the Warwickshire which contained many men from our home town of Birmingham.

Again it was to be Tom Nichols who could speak French and knew the area who told me that at many times during this period we had near squeaks and narrow escapes. In the confusion of the retreat there were times when we left a town by one road at the same time as the Germans arrived by another!

What I do recall from this period includes a tank, British or German, I still don't know which, almost running over my foot as it went through a gateway and the long hot days of what was to become a marvellous Summer. A sergeant was badly burnt, later to be first evacuated then invalidated out of the Army, after he tried to make tea on a petrol stove and a Gunner was crushed by the towing loop of a gun when a 15cwt rushing to back on to it caught his stomach. I am not sure what happened to him in the end.

Then still only a Gunner I knew only what I could see and even if my officers knew more than me, this seems very unlikely given the confused situation we were in. They did not pass the information on. What a change from later on in the war when everyone involved in an action was given as much information as possible to help them do their jobs properly.

As always happens in any confused situation, rumours of all kinds flourished. It was said that we had shot up one of our own tanks as it came over the brow of a hill and I know now that at least three British tanks were destroyed by other British forces. Today this would be called a "Blue on Blue Contact".

At one point someone said that we were going past an abandoned NAAFI. Rather than leave this for the Germans our Troop Commanders filled our trucks with all kinds of "goodies", including chocolates and cigarettes. I think that they kept the "booze" for themselves though. This was a lucky break as the chocolate biscuits which we obtained from here formed our staple food for the rest of the retreat. Our only supplies were these and a "lovely" tin of bacon which we were later to be given by an infantryman in Wormhoudt.

By now units of all kinds were becoming broken up. Our parent unit, the 48th South Midland Division was part of the rearguard of the B.E.F. Orders came down to us, somehow, I don't know how, for my own 210 Battery with two troops from 211 Battery at a later stage - to hold Wormhoudt. This was to provide time for other units of the B.E.F. to march North to the sea and Dunkirk.

On the very dull, damp and dreary night of 27th May 1940, 210 Battery with other units including that of the 2nd Royal Warwickshire Regiment arrived in Wormhoudt. On the outskirts of the town orders were given to dig in and camouflage our guns, the town was to be held at all cost to buy time for other units to escape to the sea.

My own gun was not in a very good position. We positioned it near a café so that it pointed down a road and even though we did the best we could in the time allowed, it was still very visible. Tom Nichols and his gun crew were much luckier however, their gun was in a back garden just over the road from us.

The following morning having tried to grab what sleep we could during the rest of the night the town was deathly silent. The lull before the storm. None of us then realised just how serious was our position for by now we in the town had been almost totally surrounded by the Germans from what I now know to have been the 2nd Panzer Division with elements from the S.S., comprising the Leibstandarte Adolf Hitler which was not then a Panzer Division in its own right. These men were fanatical Nazis and were to give "no quarter" whenever and wherever they fought.

The Front Line in France - 28th, 31st May 1940

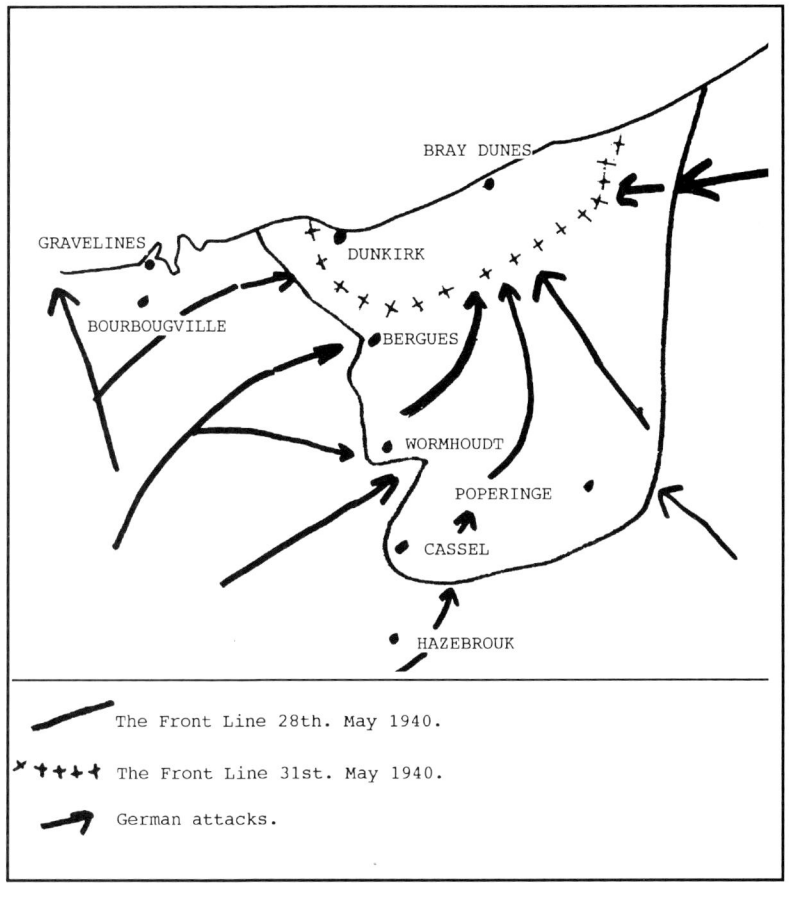

For the moment though it was quiet. One or two French soldiers in what we thought of as very old-fashioned looking uniforms wandered about rather aimlessly. Overhead was a German spotter plane, possibly Fieseler Storch which looked rather like our own R.A.F. Lysander circled but we saved our ammunition and did not fire at it. Sergeant Whistle who was my Troop Commander paid a visit to the café near us, he emerged with a number of bottles of Champagne. Being then only 20 he felt that I was too young to drink very much and would only give me just one very small glass. What a contrast this is with the situation now as regards to drinking?

Suddenly things started to happen. A French policeman began to cross the road to the café and was shot. He looked in a "bad way" as he was carried inside. What became of him later I don't know. Did he survive?

Now German mortars began to "lob" their bombs towards us and these landed increasingly nearer as time went on. Stukas, primed with information gained by a spotter plane began to attack the town in very steep dives. At times they flew so low that the heads of the pilot and air gunner could clearly be seen.

About 200 yards away down the road from us a tank fired one shell and some infantry were seen to cross the road. We took aim at the tank but, at this critical moment, and in spite of all the care and attention that our gun had received, it jammed and would not fire. This meant that most of our firepower had gone! I lay in the road and fired my Bren Gun at the Germans further down and they stumbled and fell. The mortars continued to fire, they had not stopped for one moment. I think that they were aiming at an abandoned 15cwt truck just past us and now for the first time the tank fired. With the roar of an express train a shell from it came towards us. What use was my Bren Gun against the armour of a tank? I took cover quickly.

By now we were totally on our own. No officer, no wireless and no vehicle just a gun crew with some small arms and a useless gun. Even if our truck driver had not already taken our truck to try and find Head Quarters it would not have been possible or safe to try and use it. We could do nothing more. The troop went into a huddle at the rear of the café and the decision was made that it was now, "every man for himself"!

From further down the road came the sound of the tank as it came towards us. An infantryman said that a possible way out lay through the cemetery some 50 yards or so to our rear. The decision to try it was made in seconds. Two or three of us got to our feet and ran bank, first through the cemetery then into the fields beyond it. At any moment we expected to be shot either by the Germans behind us or by our own infantry who now lay ahead of us with rifles ready.

I still don't know how we made it. After charging first through the cemetery then through several open fields we came to a farmhouse which was now full of our own infantry. On the stove a pot of coffee was still hot, this I think had been made by the owners who had left, very, very hurriedly, just before we arrived. We also came upon Major Wiggin standing outside with tears streaming down his face. He was glad to see us as until then he had believed that we had either been killed or captured.

Major Wiggin told us to join up with the infantry and took command of the party, a mixture of both gunners and infantry. That evening was wet, a very heavy shower of rain which luckily for us provided cover as we began the final march of some 20 or so miles back to Dunkirk.

I now know that after we had left Wormhoudt that the S.S. shot many of the wounded whom we had left behind and also others whom they had taken prisoner, these were mainly men of the Warwickshire Regiment. It was said that this was a form of retaliation, one of our guns had destroyed the staff car of their commander, Josef "Sepp" Dietrich, he had during World War One been Adolph Hitler's Sergeant Major and was like all his men a fanatical Nazi. Dietrich managed to escape and had to hide in a ditch for several hours.

We marched back to Dunkirk both by day and night. By day the Stukas were everywhere, bombing anything that moved on the roads. At one point, scared stiff and so hoping to be missed by them, with an old French civilian, I sheltered in a house doorway. All the time the hairs on the backs of our necks were standing up on end but we did not fully realise just what danger we were in. Everywhere now lay the debris of defeat, burnt-out and abandoned transport for all kinds, cars, trucks, motorcycles, smashed radios, equipment of all types that had taken months to make, either bombed by the Germans or smashed by our own men so that the enemy could not make use of it.

Someone told me that there were "supplies" in the rear of one truck, I crossed over to it and was able to fill my pockets and pouches with cigarettes - these kept me going for some weeks. Someone else, I can't remember who, also said that in the back of an 8cwt truck that we had left at Wormhoudt were not only many thousands of French Francs but also our Army Pay Books, Army Form 64. Still, who cared for at the time money was of no use to us.

Eventually we reached Dunkirk. Passing along a street I noticed that in a blown out shop-window were many tins of lobster. Not having then eaten for some time I collected a number of tins. It was not as it later turned out worth my effort. When we finally did managed to open them the "meat" turned out to be dry, tasteless and horrible. What a let-down!

The beaches were reached late at night. Here I met up with an old friend from school who had been serving in 212 Battery. He greeted me with the news that until then he had believed that I had been killed and was glad to see me again, alive if not safe and well. That night we "bedded down" in the sand dunes and used our "tin hats" as pillows, sleeping wherever we could find room.

When we woke up the following morning what sights met our eyes. A huge cloud of smoke from the burning oil storage tanks in Dunkirk docks rose many thousands of feet into the sky and acted as a magnet for the Luftwaffe. One the sand lay many dead men, discarded equipment of all kinds and numerous rifles. Some of the party I was with, until then unarmed, collected up one or two of them on the grounds that any weapon was better than none at all. Out to sea which was calm and as placid as a millpond were listing and burning ships and boats of all kinds.

Now men began to form orderly queues and waded out into the sea, waist deep, shoulder deep, even chin deep. A number of small boats, cabin cruisers, yachts, even rowing boats came inshore to pick them up. I joined one of the queues with my friend just in front of me. He was the first to be picked up then it was my turn. Somehow I managed to scramble aboard some sort of small craft and was taken out to where a larger boat, possibly a coaster, waited off shore.

Suddenly a massive bang, quite unlike the sound of our own guns, shook the boat I was on and I thought we had been hit by a bomb and that I would have to abandon ship. Luckily someone told me that it was just one of the ship's guns opening fire on the German aircraft above us. The sailors were marvellous, providing us with huge mugs of hot, sweet tea and massive corned beef sandwiches which we needed, not having eaten properly for some days. Every inch of space both above and below decks was filled with soldiers and the ship was to say the very least, like a "sardine tin". As we sailed back to England I thought what a very, very easy prey we would be for any U-boat that was in the area.

CHAPTER FIVE
The Regiment Reforms

One of the survivors of the B.E.F. after the disaster that was the 1940 campaign in France and Belgium, I landed in England in a South coast port sometime on either the 31st May or 1st June 1940. Of my regiment which had gone to France only in January some 540 strong, only 348 of us came home. The rest were missing in France and Belgium either killed or as captives in German hands and these would not be released until 1945. With us we brought back only what would we could carry, our total of 48 2lb Anti-Tank guns forming just a part of the 509 of this weapon alone lost in a few short weeks.

Back in England great haste was made to clear the ports of returning troops. Special trains were laid on and one took me with many other men, gunners, infantry, tanks, sappers and service corps, all mixed up together to near Derby to a reception centre where we were to be documented and then "posted back" to where our units were reforming. On every station platform people of all ages waited with food and drinks, it was as if "we had won the war", not been defeated. As soon as I could I let my folks know that I was safe and this was a great relief to them.

Looking back it seems very strange that though I was now what the American's would call "a combat veteran", in law I was still a minor, not reaching the age of 21 until 13th September 1940.

The Worcestershire Yeomanry was reforming in Devon around Okehampton with 210 Battery nearby in Bere Alston. It was here that I was billeted with a friend in the home of a local teacher. Like so many places in England in rural areas at this time, mains electricity and gas had not reached the town and so most families cooked on small oil-fuelled stoves.

The time that we spent in this area was a very happy one for me, I well remember attending many dances in the Village Hall, it was here that we also had to stand guard duty and the time that two Sergeants known as Sergeant Black and Sergeant White returned home rather the worse for wear one night after sampling the "local brew". One of them then found out the hard way that he had lost his false teeth but found them in the road the following morning! Another time a pre-war member of the battery was being discharged from the Army to return to his now, reserved occupation.

He left the town mimicking the rather "posh" voice of one of our officers as he went much to the officer's fury but there was then nothing he could do about it.

Though the Regiment was anti-tank artillery Britain was at this time so short of weapons that the first we were issued with were Pikes, just Bayonets fixed it to pipes. How we would have fared with these if the Germans had invaded I am glad not to have found out! What was to make the general loss of weapons even worse was the bombing by the Germans of the Birmingham Small Arms factory in Small Heath, Birmingham some months later. This was kept a very close secret as it was here that all the Lee Enfield Rifles made in England were produced. The first real weapons which we were later to receive were very old 6lb guns released from storage by the Royal Navy who had kept them to arm merchant ships. Though during World War One this type of weapon had been used to very good effect as the main armament in the first tanks by now they were rather "past it", besides being rather heavy and cumbersome to move quickly. These were replaced by another World War One gun the French 75mm Field Gun. Though both of these types of gun fired with loud bangs they were not as effective in the Anti-Tank role as our old and much loved 2lbs had been. We were so glad when production allowed us to receive these again but this was not for a number of months.

The Regiment was now allocated to "Home Defence" duties as part of "Home Forces" and trained on Dartmoor often going to Cornwall for exercises on Bodmin Moor with other troops. Food at this time was very good. Often in Devon we would be given for our meal breaks very large, doorstep thick, cheese sandwiches and gallons of hot sweet tea while in Cornwall these were replaced by real Cornish Pasties, the type that you could not and still can't get anywhere else outside the county. Ideal food for young fit and active men who were burning off energy at a great rate.

On the Moors it was often cold and foggy and difficult to see for any distance ahead. A trick that some people often played to delay our return to billets and thus our availability for fatigues, was to drop into the petrol tank on our vehicles a small piece of cotton waste. This would make its way into the carburettor and stop the engine. By the time this had been cleared and we had "finally" returned to base time was only left for the vehicles and guns to be cleaned and a hot meal eaten before we could fall exhausted into our beds being too tired to do anything else.

Between our various exercises and my duties I had a very near miss on the "personal front". Somehow I became engaged to be married and even bought a ring for my then intended. Luckily this fell through and she ended up married to a local bus driver instead! I also well remember a lighter event from this time when one evening I and a few friends heard a nun who had a superb voice singing the Ave Maria. Even now when I hear this I am taken back to that time.

Being a "Home Forces" unit the Regiment was in constant flux with both officers and men being posted in and out and going away on training courses. I was now a full Corporal or Bombardier and someone, I would still like to know who, decided that I should attend a Sergeants course on Anglesey.

The course did not go at all well for me. One day we attended a lecture sitting down in a field that contained a large number of very inquisitive young cattle. The lecture over and having "marched out" of it for a tea break, I realised that something was missing from my belt, this turned out to be my Bayonet. Any loss of a weapon being treated as a most severe offence I was forced to return and look for it before I was "found out". I don't like cattle at any time especially not in the numbers present in that field! Shaking inwardly I returned and was so glad when I found it and was able to "beat a hasty retreat", most of the cows by now having decided that their "fun" for the day was over and had gone well away.

On another day a very senior officer was present when we were engaged in throwing "live" grenades. He felt that I had not ducked down far enough to escape possible flying fragments and made the comment that he questioned how I would fare in action. As I had been at Dunkirk some months before and felt I knew all about the effects of grenades, I very stupidly told him this. The result was that after he had gone a nice shade of purple I had my name taken for insolence. This combined with my bad handwriting and spelling so that I failed the course and was sent back to the Regiment at my existing rank marked "not suitable for further promotion".

The Worcestershire Yeomanry now formed part of the 42nd Armoured Division, and moved to Yorkshire where it was to train for many months on the Pennines. I spent very little time with it after my return from my course as the constant lifting of heavy weights, guns and ammunition, resulted in a slipped disk in my back. In great pain I was sent to hospital and thus ended over two, on the whole, happy years of service in both war and peace. This was later to result in the downgrading of my medical category and my eventual discharge on medical grounds from the Army.

CHAPTER SIX
Hospital and Romance

The first hospital that I was sent to was in Harrogate a spa town in North Yorkshire some 10 miles south of Ripon. Then and still to some lesser extent now, Harrogate was regarded as "rather posh" being full of well to do retired people. My first treatment was daily baths in the famous spa water, this both tasted and smelt totally vile almost as if it came from a sewer. Some people I know swear by it as a treatment for various ailments, me, I swear about it.

The spa treatment failed so I was then transferred to a former mental hospital near Manchester for further treatment including an operation on my back. Like so many similar establishments this hospital had on the outbreak of war been taken over by the Emergency Medical Service for the treatment of wounds and injuries of both civilians and service people and had a fully civilian staff of doctors and nurses. Some of the previous mental patients remained in one distant part of the hospital and at night and especially when there was a full moon, we could hear them shouting and screaming. It was here that I was to spend the next nine months.

The doctor who dealt with those of us with spinal problems and who was the one who actually operated on me was a "left over" from before the war. He had the habit of on his morning rounds greeting us with, "Good Evening," then on his evening rounds with, "Good Morning,". A further habit of his was to hold his pocket watch on its long chain in front of us and he talked. We wondered if this was an attempt to hypnotise us and dated back to his pre-war treatment of mental patients whom he may have tried to "calm down" by this means.

Occupational therapy at this hospital consisted of making leather handbags. A very profitable process this was as the nurses provided a ready market for all we could make.

As a former mental hospital well away from the city centre the hospital had extensive grounds. These were put to very effective use being dug up and used to grow all kinds of fruit and vegetables which we later ate. We were as a consequence hungry though when we had visitors, they was usually the case, always bring us in either extra food or cigarettes. It was through this that I met Alice who used to bring in meat-pies.

Alice was 28 years of age and lived in Manchester where she was separated from her husband. She took a size 3 in shoes and when out always wore a coat with a fur collar which was then the very height of fashion. Always bubbly and cheerful she was another Gracie Fields with a good voice which she continually used to sing the popular songs of the time. Songs like, "San Francisco", and "Some day you will miss me honey". Sweet and sickly they may be to "modern ears" these were the songs that we sang through the dark days of the war.

When at last I was allowed to walk again and was given a pass from the hospital for an evening out I met her in a pub near to Old Trafford and she bought me a drink. As I had not been discharged from hospital and was still in the Army I had to wear my hospital blues to show that I was injured and undergoing treatment. These consisted of a blue suit with a white shirt and a red tie and had to be worn by all those who were patients when out of the hospital grounds, unless we were engaged in sports when our proper uniforms could be worn. Somehow, I don't think for one moment that what we got up to later could then be regarded as sports, though people today may have a different opinion.

When the pub finally shut that first magical evening, I walked Alice home to her house in Duke Street even though this did mean that I then missed my last tram back to the hospital. Here Alice first opened the front door and then asked me inside. Once in she stood in the dim light of a banked up coal-fire in the rear downstairs room and very slowly undressed until all she wore was her short chemise. Now she looked at me in a particular way that women have and told be that if I behaved myself I could stay the night. What could I do? I took her in my arms and we went upstairs together and made love.

Finally, I just had to leave and walked back to the hospital through the total darkness of the blacked-out streets. Very luckily for me some of my friends had covered up my absence. A kit bag had been put in my bed so it seemed to a casual glance that I had been in my bed asleep all the time. It was true that I had been in bed but not that one and as to sleep?

After the first magical evening together Alice gave me a key to her house and we met whenever we could even after I was transferred to an Army convalescent hospital which was still in Manchester. One night we attended a "get together" there. Though everyone was trying to have a "good time" things were slow and rather staid until I managed to get her to sing. Then what a change as she sang all the then popular songs, people on their feet cheering and clapping and not wanting her to stop. It went on and on for what seemed hours.

The next morning though it was a different matter. I was ordered to report to the Matron's Office. Matron was like all hospital matrons of this time, military or civilian, a real dragon. She gave me one of the worst "dressing downs" that I have ever had for allowing and encouraging Alice to sing. Some of the terms included, "not what we are used to," and "an utter disgrace," and "should be ashamed of yourself."

Possibly it was due to this escapade that led to my discharge soon afterwards and I was forced to leave the area and lost touch with Alice as a consequence.

Some time later I did manage to return to where Alice had lived in Duke Street, but it was to find her gone. The person who then was living in her old house told me that after I had left Alice died after she had managed to get a chicken bone stuck in her throat.

Even though many years have now passed I still miss her.

Chorley Hospital Staff
Sister Doherty on the left

CHAPTER SEVEN
178 Battery and Demobilisation

When I was finally and fully discharged from hospital the problems that I had had with my back now meant a downgrading in my medical category from A1 to B. This also meant that not now fit for "active" front line service, I had to leave the Worcestershire Yeomanry and be posted to a unit that was not likely to serve overseas.

The unit in which I eventually found myself was the 178 Anti-Aircraft Battery based at Chorley in Lancashire. Part of the home based Anti-Aircraft Command it was armed and equipped with Bofors 40mm light Anti-Aircraft guns at a time when the air-raids on Britain were almost totally over.

To my biased eyes 178 Battery was neither as smart or as efficient as 210 Battery from which I had come and in which many of my friends still then served. When I first arrived I was a full corporal or Bombardier still but was soon demoted after I had felt unwell and unwisely had an argument with a sergeant. Shade of my experiences at Anglesey again!

To start with I was based with the other members of my "then" gun crew sleeping in a hut in which we had a small stove for both heating and cooking purposes. One day a member of the crew suggested that chicken would make a change from our rations with which we had been issued. The night saw two of us walking for what seemed miles and miles over fields and ended up in a chicken run where the other chap managed to grab a chicken and wring its neck. Careful not to leave a trail of feathers we returned to our hut where the chicken was roasted for dinner the next night. It was as hard as an old boot and almost impossible to eat. The same man when acting as cook also later tried to make a rice pudding. As anyone who has ever made a rice pudding will know, only a small quantity of rice is required as it soaks up so much liquid. Unfortunately for us the man concerned did not know this! He put far, far too much rice into the pudding and then as it cooked, had to spend some time skimming it off the surface of the pudding.

For a time I was billeted in the same house as a sergeant and together we used to go out for a drink when our duties were over for the day. It was through this that I met the daughter of the local solicitor who taught me a number of new dance steps, then later a nurse at the local hospital called Sister Dougherty.

One night after I had been out with Sister Dougherty, I missed the last bus and then in the black-out managed to run full tilt into a lamp post, breaking all of the glass that until that moment had remained in the lamp and my glasses at the same time. Taken to the casualty unit of the hospital where the Sister was now on duty to be checked over, I was only found to be heavily bruised. When I was brought in Sister Dougherty went as white as a sheet but dare not say anything or she would have been in trouble with the hospital authorities.

The sequel to this event was that having been "checked over" an officer on a motorbike gave me a lift back to my billet. The next morning, bruised and battered as I was I was charged with being out without a pass the night before. Like many a man before me and I expect since as well, I had been caught doing something which we all did even though we knew what the consequences would be if and when we were finally caught!

During 1943 having served in the Territorial Army from 1937 to 1939 and in the Army as a full-time soldier since 1939, over 4_ years in total, I was demobilised on medical grounds and returned to my home in Birmingham. At first as a consequence of the injury to my back I was granted a small disability pension of 20% but this was later reduced when a "grateful government" decided that my disability was not due to war service? After many letters over a long period of time I managed to get this restored but the amount of money due to me from the time when this was reduced was not made up.

In addition to the problems which I had and still have with my back I am, like many other gunners, partly deaf. They hearing in my ears being damaged by the sound of gunfire over long periods. I do not get any form of pension for this even though this was caused by my war service.

Wormhoudt Cemetery - April 1998

Grave of Gunner Edkins
Worcestershire Yeomanry

CHAPTER EIGHT
Civilian Life - Return to Wormhoudt

When in 1943 I was finally discharged from the Army the war in Europe still had two more long and bitter years to run.

It may sound strange to today's young people and others facing unemployment but at this time there was not only full employment but even a great shortage of man and woman power, every fit man and woman not involved in essential activities being in the armed forces. As such I very quickly was able to find work on my return to Birmingham where I took up a position as a Rate Fixer with the firm of Fisher and Ludlow. It was here that I was soon to meet the one who was to become my beloved wife.

At this time Fisher and Ludlow were busy making all kinds and all sizes of nut and bolt, mainly for the aircraft industry. My soon to be wife Gladys was employed by them as a Progress Chaser and we first met when she used to make tea for myself and other rate fixers who passed through her department.

Gladys and I soon became engaged and were married on 20th June 1945 at Quinton Parish Church in Hagley Road West, Birmingham and were to have 53 very happy years together. All through our life together we kept our marriage vows of, "for richer for poorer in sickness and in health," and had three children who have grown up without the need to don uniforms and defend our way of life and for this I am very thankful. Gladys was always very interested in my experiences at Wormhoudt and shortly before she died I began to note down my experiences for her.

After I left Fisher and Ludlow I had a number of different jobs including working as a glass cutter for a well known local company in Smethwick, a period in the library at what is now the University of Aston and a longish period working for the Hoover Company in Birmingham. Together we also took over and ran a Transport Café on Hagley Road West, this is now the Studio Restaurant. We had our "ups and downs" as is usual in any relationship but she cared for me even when I became ill with bladder problems and was ill for a number of years, this as well as looking after three growing children.

Gladys died on 22nd December 1998 and I have placed a memorial to her in the church where we were married in Quinton,

Birmingham. This is the church that I now attend on a more regular basis than I did previously while she was still alive.

Some few months before Gladys died, my son took both Gladys and myself and our Grandchildren to France. It was April 1998 and very cold and damp and the first time I had returned since 1940.

Unlike when I had first gone to France in January 1940 and returned in May 1940 we did not travel in an overcrowded troopship or on a "cargo boat", but in the comfort of a train through the Channel Tunnel. On reflection I am so glad that the Channel Tunnel did not exist in 1940 for I am sure that had it done so the Germans would have used it to invade our shores.

Wormhoudt like so many places in Northern France that were devastated during the campaigns of 1940 and 1944 was rebuilt long ago and few signs of the fighting remain. The people remember though as we found out when I needed to buy a warm jacket and on telling the owner of this shop that I had been at Wormhoudt, he presented us with a bottle of wine as a token of his personal thanks.

When a local resident in Wormhoudt realised that we were from England he told us that where my gun had been the S.S. later stripped and shot a number of men, I now believe that these were fellow gunners from my Regiment, Baxter, Edkins and Bowns. Gunner Baxter managed to escape and returned to England via Dunkirk but what became of the others I have no knowledge. When I told him that I had been there he marvelled at my survival. We visited the Civil Cemetery in Wormhoudt, the cemetery near to where my gun had been positioned and through which I had run to escape. Here we found the gunners of both 210 and 211 Battery as well as men from other units in graves well cared for by the Commonwealth War Graves Commission. Near to them in a Cross of Sacrifice. Well does the symbol of the Crusaders Sword on the cross reflect what they did, they died fighting against evil!

APPENDIX 1
Details of the Worcestershire Yeomanry
1920 - 1942

1920
The Regiment was reformed as a "horsed" cavalry unit after World War One.

1922
The Regiment was transferred to the Royal Artillery and became a Field Artillery Regiment with 18lb Field Guns.
It was "brigaded" with the Oxfordshire Yeomanry.
The headquarters of the Regiment was transferred from Worcester to Kidderminster.

1924
The first post-World War One firing camp took place at Okehampton.

1928 - 1930
Mechanisation began with the horses being replaced by Morris 6 wheeled tractors to pull the guns.

1938
The Regiment had its role changed from Field to Anti-Tank Artillery and the 18lb Field Guns were replaced by 2lb Anti-Tank Guns.
On renaming the new Regiment became the 53rd, Worcestershire and Oxfordshire Yeomanry Anti-Tank Regiment Royal Artillery Territorial Army.

1939
Renamed yet again the Worcestershire Yeomanry became the 53rd, Anti-Tank Regiment Royal Artillery Territorial Army and lost its links with the Oxfordshire Yeomanry.
On the 1st September and Regiment was mobilised for "war service".
War was declared on 3rd September 1939.

The Regiment moved to Wantage in Oxfordshire to begin extensive training and be brought up to strength in both men and equipment.

1940

Part now of the 48th (South Midland) Division the Regiment was ordered to France in January where it joined the British Expeditionary Force.

When the "phoney war" ended and the German attack on France and Belgium began the Regiment was one of the first to advance into Belgium.

Forming part of the rearguard of the British Expeditionary Force the Regiment was in action at both Wormhoudt and Cassel.

After the loss of all its guns the survivors of the Regiment reached England via Dunkirk and Operation Dynamo.

Reorganisation and refitting of the Regiment began in Wiltshire and Devon where it now operated as a Home Defence Regiment.

1941

The Regiment was moved from Wiltshire and Devon to the North of England where it undertook training in the Pennines for many months.

The parent formation to which the Regiment now belonged was the 42nd Armoured Division.

1942

The Regiment began to have its 2lb Anti-Tank guns replaced by the newer and more effective 6lb Anti-Tank guns capable of defeating even the frontal armour of all German tanks then in operation.

APPENDIX 2
Weapons including Small Arms

In 1939 the War Office scale of equipment to be held by a Royal Artillery Anti-Tank Regiment of 540 all ranks consisted of:

2lb Anti-Tank Guns	48.
Boy(e)s Anti-Tank Rifles .55	13.
Bren Light Machine Guns .303 (7.7mm)	66.
Lee-Enfield Rifles .303 (7.7mm)	182.
Pistols/revolvers usually either:-	
Enfield No 2 Mk 1 .38 (9mm)	
Webley No 1 Mk 6 .455	77.

The ACTUAL issue of weapons to the Regiment at that time was rather different and was:-

2lb Anti-Tank Guns	4.
Boy(e)s Anti-Tank Rifles .55	4.
Bren Light Machine Guns .303 (7.7mm)	4.
Lee-Enfield Rifles .303 (7.7mm)	48.
Pistols/revolvers usually either:-	
Enfield No 2 Mk 1 .38 (9mm)	
Webley No 1 Mk 6 .455	0.

Note: The totals of pistols and revolvers given above does not include any that were personal weapons and which had been purchased privately by officers and or senior N.C.O.s.

APPENDIX 3
The 2lb Anti-Tank Gun

2lb Anti-Tank Gun shown in the towing position

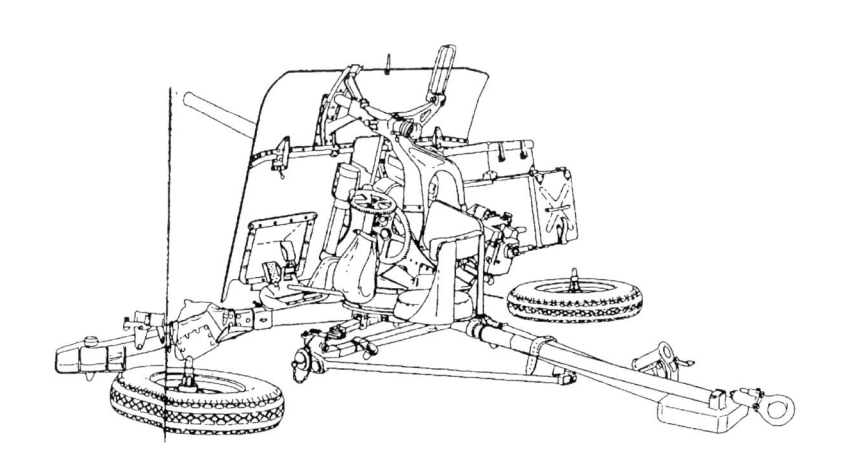

2lb Anti-Tank Gun shown set up and ready for action

The 2lb Anti-Tank Gun

Though always known as the 2lb Anti-Tank gun this weapon actually fired a solid shot weighing some 2_ pounds.

In the 1930's the "then" tactical doctrine called for a small, light, high velocity, quick firing weapon which could be quickly and easily be taken into the brought out of action. Weapons of this generation included both the U.S. and German 37mm Anti-Tank guns. Though very similar in actual penetrative power to both of these weapons the British designed gun was much heavier and more cumbersome and was mounted on a cruciform platform to give all round traverse, something which both the U.S. and German guns lacked. The gun could either be towed by or mounted "portee" on the back of a small 15cwt lorry and this often took place in the Western Desert campaigns of 1940-1942. It could be and was also sometimes manhandled into position.

Until the middle of 1942 when it was replaced by the British designed 6lb Anti-Tank gun, the 2lb Anti-Tank gun formed the main weapon of all British and Empire Anti-Tank Regiments. Until this time it also served as the main gun on all British designed Infantry and Cruiser Tanks. For the entire period of the Second World War the 2lb Anti-Tank gun remained the main armament of some British designed Armoured cars.

Initially an excellent weapon more than capable of penetrating even the frontal armour on all German Tanks then in service an increase in both the thickness of their armour and the introduction of angled surfaces soon meant that it became ineffective except at suicidal close range. The Germans had quickly learnt the lesson taught to them at Arras in 1940 when the 7th, Panzer Division took very heavy losses when the 2lb Anti-Tank guns were used against them.

Due to the very heavy losses of all forms of weapons at Dunkirk in 1940 and the problems that would have been caused if the factories had tried to change production to the heavier weapon, the 6lb Anti-Tank gun, during 1940, a decision was made that "any gun is better than none". This decision was to have very dire consequences and led to the loss of many men, gunners and tank crews alike, forced to continue to use what was now an outdated weapon.

Even when the 2lb Anti-Tank gun was finally replaced by a heavier weapon in the Western Desert and in Western Europe it was still effective in dealing with the lighter and less well armoured Italian tanks.

When in action against the Japanese in the Far East from December 1941 the 2lb Anti-Tank gun remained a very effective weapon. The few Japanese tanks that operated had only thin armour and this could be and was easily penetrated all through the war. A further use for this weapon was in the "bunker busting" role. Comparatively light in weight it could be and was often transported easily through the jungle where its solid shot was most effective against enemy bunkers.

One of the main disadvantages which the 2lb Anti-Tank gun faced all through its service life was its total inability to fire any ammunition other than a solid shot. It could not fire an explosive shell and thus was unable to be of any use in an Infantry support role where high explosive was required.

APPENDIX 4
Shot and Shell

At its most basic a shot is very like, but is much larger than a standard rifle bullet. It is a sold mass of metal that does not contain any explosive and is akin in operation to the old round cannon balls. In action it relies for its effect on its weight or mass and the speed or velocity at which it is fired.

When used in the armour piercing role a solid shot is usually made from a very hard steel or other material, often in World War Two Tungsten but now depleted Uranium is used. It has been proved many times that a small, hard very fast flying shot will penetrate armour where a larger, slower and less hard one will fail.

Once a solid shot has penetrated armour it uses its own momentum to destroy anything in its path. It has been again proved many times that to defeat solid shot the armour which it faces must either be of sufficient thickness or hardness to stop it or as it is now very common, angled from the vertical. Shot hitting anything other than a vertical surface will often ricochet off and do no damage.

An explosive shell differs from a solid shot by being a comparatively thin container containing some form of high explosive. Usually shaped to reduce wind resistance as it flies through the air it can be timed to explode either on contact, when it has passed through armour or at a set time. Once through an armour plate the explosion will destroy anything in the immediate area.

When used against tanks or other armoured vehicles it can be, like the solid shot, defeated by thick armour or angled armour which will cause it to explode prematurely before it has penetrated. However, due to the explosive content of the shell and the "splinters" which are formed by the explosion blowing apart its casing it is very effective against infantry and any who are not "dug in" and protected against the flying fragments or the force of the explosion.

APPENDIX 5
Insignia

During the Second World War, insignia that was worn by every service man or woman on the arm consisted of, from the top downwards, of the following.
1. Corps or regimental shoulder badge. Sometimes, usually just only in the early part of the War these were made of brass which had to be very highly polished. Later and more usually in service the brass was replaced by a cloth flash on which was embroidered the name of the unit to which a man or woman belonged.
2. The Divisional Flash. This bore the badge of the parent division to which a man or woman belonged and was always made of cloth.
3. The Arm of Service Strip. A rectangular bar of cloth in the one, two or three colours of one's particular arm of service.
4. Any N.C.O. or Warrant Officer badges of rank. In the case of N.C.O.s these were white downward pointing chevrons on a khaki background.

Shoulder Flash of the Royal Artillery
In cloth, this consisted of a blue background the words "Royal Artillery" in red.

48th, South Midland Division Flash
On a dark blue oval was first set a red diamond in which in blue was a Macaw.
This was a first-line Territorial Army Division composed of members of the Territorial Army from the counties of Gloucestershire, Berkshire, Buckinghamshire, Warwickshire and Worcestershire. In 1940 it formed part of the B.E.F. in France then from 1942 onwards was a United Kingdom based training division.

42nd, Armoured Division
Inside an equal sided large red diamond was a smaller and equal-sided white diamond.
This division formed in 1941 when the then 42nd, East Lancashire Division was converted to an armoured Division. It took over the existing badge of this division and until disbanded in 1943 served in the United Kingdom as a training unit.

Arm of Service Strip of the Royal Artillery
A two inch in length strip of coloured cloth that of the Royal Artillery was from the left, red then blue.

APPENDIX 6
Conscription and National Service

In May 1939, the War with Germany then seen to be very close, the British Government passed the first compulsory Military Service Act that had been introduced since the end of World War One. This Act, sometimes referred to as the Militia Act required that all fit men aged from 20 to 24 register for a period of military service, the first men in this age band being called up very shortly afterwards. On the German invasion of Poland on the 1st September 1939 all Military, Airforce and Naval reservists and including the members of the Territorial Army, Auxiliary Airforce and Naval Volunteer Reserve were called up for full-time service.

On the 3rd September 1939, War having been declared earlier that day, parliament met and passed the first of the National Service Acts (Armed Forces). This Act required that unless involved in reserved occupations or other work of national importance, all fit males aged 18 to 41 must register for "call up".

1941 was to see an extension of the age band liable for "call up" from between 18 and 51. All those who joined the forces under this or the earlier acts were required to serve "for the duration of the War or King's Pleasure". This was unlike the so termed, "draft" which operated in U.S.A. where the period of service was limited to the "end of the War plus six months". Many men called up under each of these acts were to see service in the Worcestershire Yeomanry.

Operational from 1st January 1948, a post-war National Service Act required those involved to serve first for 18 months, later 2 years full-time then for 4 then 3_ years part-time with an appropriate Territorial Army or other unit. This included their liability to attend their units "annual camp"! Again from this act many men were to serve post-war with the Worcestershire Yeomanry.

Conscription ended on 31st December 1960 and by the middle of 1963 all those involved had left both the full-time and part-time armed services.

Between 1939 and 1960 the total of men called up for the Army exceeded 3,800,000!

APPENDIX 7
The German Soldiers' Ten Commandments and The Waffen S.S. Oath

In the Pay Book of every German Soldier who served in the Second World War was a list of Ten Regulations which governed his conduct in War. They included the following:-
While fighting for victory the German Soldier will observe the rules of chivalrous warfare.
No enemy who has surrendered will be killed.
Prisoners of War will not be ill-treated or insulted.
While arms, maps and records are to be taken from them, their personal belongings will not be touched.
Offences against the above regulations on matters of duty will be punished.
Reprisals are only permissible on the order of Higher Commands.

The Waffen S.S. was first organised as the personal bodyguard of Adolph Hitler. Starting in 1934 and ending in 1945 every man who joined any unit of the Waffen S.S. had to swear a personal oath of loyalty to him. This stated that:-
"I swear to you, Adolph Hitler, as Fuhrer and Reichancellor, loyalty and bravery, I vow to you, and to those you have named and command me, obedience unto death, so help me God."

APPENDIX 8
The Massacre at Wormhoudt - May 1940

The killing by the Waffen S.S. from the Leibstandarte Adolf Hitler of wounded and prisoners from units of the B.E.F. including the Royal Warwickshire Regiment, was just one of a number of war crimes and atrocities which they were to be involved with in this month alone.

After the War the commander of the Leibstandarte for much of the time, including the period of May 1940, Joseph "Sepp" Dietrich was brought to trial for this crime. However, as it was proved that when the massacre took place he was still "taking cover" in a ditch after his vehicle had been destroyed, he was found not guilty.

Many of the men of the Leibstandarte at Wormhoudt were to die in later campaigns however the man responsible, so it has been said, for actually giving the order to fire and execute the wounded and prisoners was Wilhelm Mohnke who survived the War and was in 1945 the final commander of Hitler's bunker in Berlin.

The Red Army refused to hand Wilhelm Mohnke over to the "western allies" to face trial and he was detained in Soviet camps for over ten years, finally being allowed to return to West Germany during the mid-1950s. I expect that it was only this long detention in Russia that prevented him from an early morning walk with sudden and very fatal consequences for him after he had kept a date with a hangman.

The case of Mohnke is still open though and the United Nations War Crimes Commission have given him both a file and case number. It has been very strongly believed that he was either directly involved or implicated in War Crimes against citizens of Germany, Poland, Britain, France, Belgium, Canada, the U.S.A and the Soviet Union.

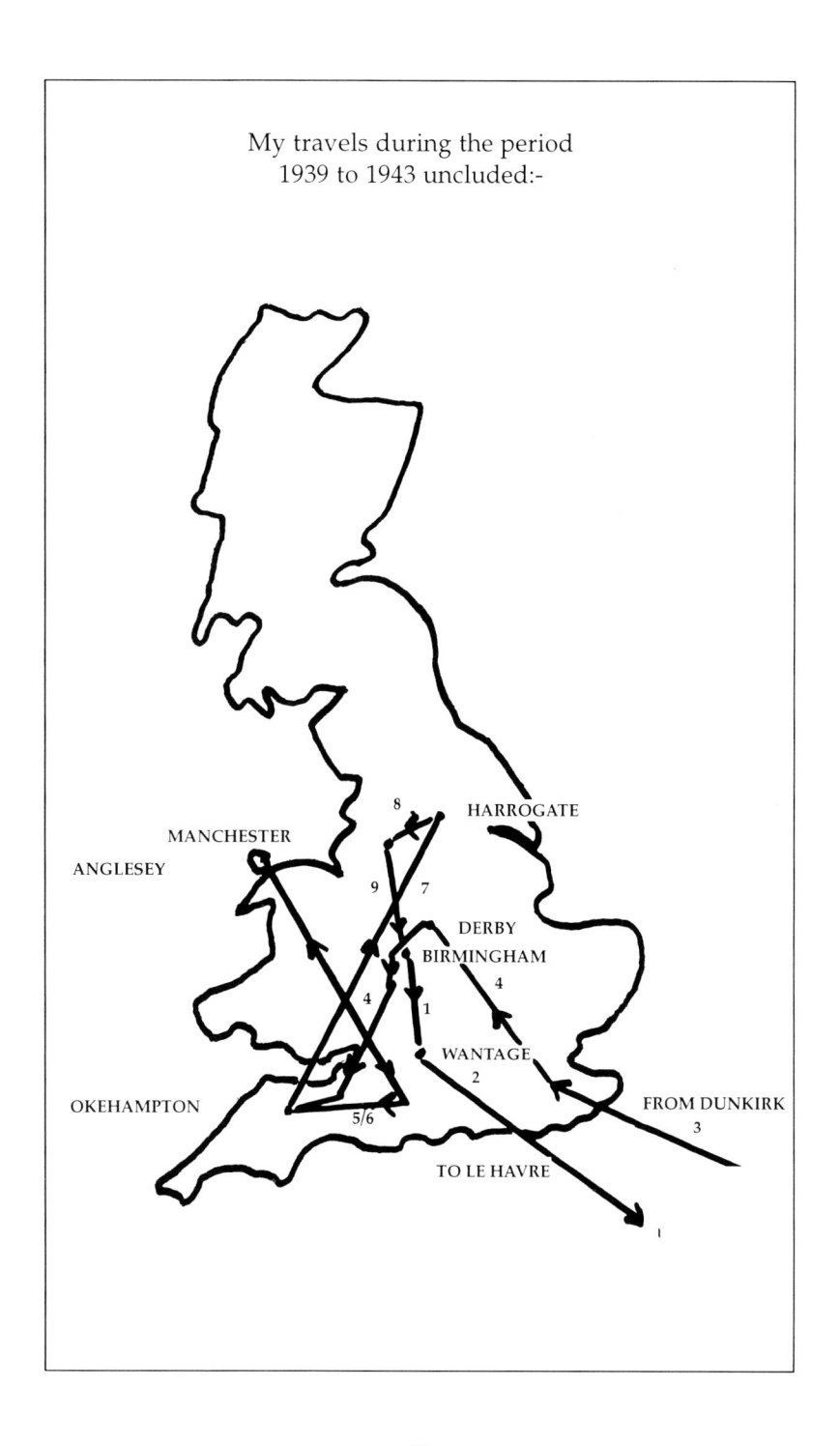

My travels during the period
1939 to 1943 uncluded:-

MANCHESTER
ANGLESEY
8
HARROGATE
9   7
DERBY
BIRMINGHAM
4
4
1
WANTAGE
2
OKEHAMPTON
5/6
FROM DUNKIRK
3
TO LE HAVRE
1

Bibliography

Hitlers Luftwaffe
By Tony Wood and Bill Gunston
I.S.B.N. 0 86101 005 1

Hitler's Last General
By Ian Sayer and Douglas Botting

British and American Infantry Weapons of World War Two
By A. J.Barker
S.B.N. 85368 489 8

France Summer 1940
By John Williams

Barrage the Guns in Action
By I.V. Hogg

The Guns 1939 - 1945
By I.V. Hogg

Heraldry in War
By Howard N. Cole

The Scourge of the Swastika
By Lord Russell of Liverpool

Pillar of Fire - Dunkirk 1940
By Ronald Atkin
I.S.B.N. 0 283 996978

Dunkirk - The Storms of War
By John Harris
I.S.B.N 0 7153 78570

Worcestershire Yeomanry Old Comrades Association notes.